PRESIDENTS

JAMES
BUCHANAN

A MyReportLinks.com Book

Jeff C. Young

 MyReportLinks.com Books

an imprint of

Enslow Publishers, Inc. E

Box 398, 40 Industrial Road
Berkeley Heights, NJ 07922
USA

To Jeff "Roget" Gorham, 1948–1983:
thank you for being a friend.

MyReportLinks.com Books, an imprint of Enslow Publishers, Inc. MyReportLinks is a trademark of Enslow Publishers, Inc.

Library of Congress Cataloging-in-Publication Data

Young, Jeff C., 1948–
    James Buchanan / Jeff C. Young.
      p. cm. — (Presidents)
    Summary: A biography of the fifteenth president of the United States, describing his attempts to lead a divided nation under the scourge of slavery. Includes Internet links to Web sites, source documents, and photographs related to James Buchanan.
    Includes bibliographical references and index.
    ISBN 0-7660-5101-3
    1. Buchanan, James, 1791–1868—Juvenile literature. 2. Presidents—United States—Biography—Juvenile literature. [1. Buchanan, James, 1791–1868. 2. Presidents.] I. Title. II. Series.
E437 .Y68 2003
973.925'092—dc21

                              2002003418
Printed in the United States of America

10 9 8 7 6 5 4 3 2 1

To Our Readers:
Through the purchase of this book, you and your library gain access to the Report Links that specifically back up this book.
The Publisher will provide access to the Report Links that back up this book and will keep these Report Links up to date on **www.myreportlinks.com** for three years from the book's first publication date.
We have done our best to make sure all Internet addresses in this book were active and appropriate when we went to press. However, the author and the Publisher have no control over, and assume no liability for, the material available on those Internet sites or on other Web sites they may link to.
The usage of the MyReportLinks.com Books Web site is subject to the terms and conditions stated on the Usage Policy Statement on **www.myreportlinks.com**.
In the future, a password may be required to access the Report Links that back up this book. The password is found on the bottom of page 4 of this book.
Any comments or suggestions can be sent by e-mail to comments@myreportlinks.com or to the address on the back cover.

Photo Credits: America's Story from America's Library/Library of Congress, p. 40; © Corel Corporation, pp. 1 (background), 3; © 1998 Missouri Historical Society, St. Louis, p. 38; © National Museum of American History, Smithsonian Institution, p. 45; Department of the Interior, p. 36; Dickinson College, p. 16; *Harper's Weekly*, pp. 30, 33; Library of Congress, pp. 1, 12, 22, 24, 26, 27, 35; Mural by Allyn Cox, p. 18; MyReportLinks.com Books, p. 4; The White House Historical Association, pp. 32, 42.

Cover Photo: © Corel Corporation; The James Buchanan Foundation

Contents

MyReportLinks.com Books
Great Books, Great Links, Great for Research!

MyReportLinks.com Books present the information you need to learn about your report subject. In addition, they show you where to go on the Internet for more information. The pre-evaluated Report Links that back up this book are kept up to date on **www.myreportlinks.com**. With the purchase of a MyReportLinks.com Books title, you and your library gain access to the Report Links that specifically back up that book. The Report Links save hours of research time and link to dozens—even hundreds—of Web sites, source documents, and photos related to your report topic.

Please see "To Our Readers" on the Copyright page for important information about this book, the MyReportLinks.com Books Web site, and the Report Links that back up this book.

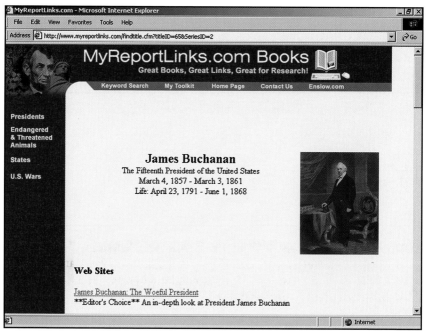

Access:

The Publisher will provide access to the Report Links that back up this book and will try to keep these Report Links up to date on our Web site for three years from the book's first publication date. Please enter **PBU3095** if asked for a password.

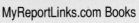
Report Links

The Internet sites described below can be accessed at
http://www.myreportlinks.com

*EDITOR'S CHOICE

▶ **James Buchanan: The Woeful President**
This Web site provides a comprehensive biography of James Buchanan.
Here you will learn about his life, family, presidency, domestic and
foreign policy, and his legacy.

Link to this Internet site from http://www.myreportlinks.com

*EDITOR'S CHOICE

▶ **James Buchanan**
At this Web site you will find facts and figures about James Buchanan,
including presidential election results, a list of his cabinet members,
historical documents, and other Internet resources.

Link to this Internet site from http://www.myreportlinks.com

*EDITOR'S CHOICE

▶ **"I Do Solemnly Swear . . ."**
At this Web site you will find memorabilia from James Buchanan's
Inauguration Day, including images, his inaugural address, and a
journal entry from Montgomery C. Meigs.

Link to this Internet site from http://www.myreportlinks.com

*EDITOR'S CHOICE

▶ **The American Presidency: James Buchanan**
This biography of James Buchanan provides an in-depth look at the
issues that shaped his presidency. You will also learn about his early life
and political career, rise to national leadership, and about how
Buchanan is looked upon historically.

Link to this Internet site from http://www.myreportlinks.com

*EDITOR'S CHOICE

▶ **The American President: "The Professional Politician"**
This PBS Web site includes profiles of four presidents, including James
Buchanan, who were thought to be "professional politicians." You
will also find an audio clip discussing Buchanan's lack of leadership in
the 1850s.

Link to this Internet site from http://www.myreportlinks.com

*EDITOR'S CHOICE

▶ **Objects from the Presidency**
At this site you will find information on all the presidents of the
United States, including James Buchanan. Read a brief description of
the era he lived in, and learn about the office of the presidency.

Link to this Internet site from http://www.myreportlinks.com

Back   Forward   Stop   Review   Home   Explore   Favorites   History

Report Links

 The Internet sites described below can be accessed at
http://www.myreportlinks.com

▶**American Presidents: Life Portraits: James Buchanan**
At this Web site you will find "Life Facts" and "Did you know?" trivia
about James Buchanan. You will also find a letter written by Buchanan
to his brother and links to his birthplace and gravesite.

Link to this Internet site from http://www.myreportlinks.com

▶**The American Presidency: John C. Breckinridge**
A brief profile of James Buchanan's vice president, John C. Breckinridge.
Learn about Breckinridge's political career and civil service.

Link to this Internet site from http://www.myreportlinks.com

▶**American Votes: James Buchanan**
This Web site, from the Duke University Special Collections Library, features
an 1856 James Buchanan campaign poster.

Link to this Internet site from http://www.myreportlinks.com

▶**Buchanan's Birthplace**
A brief description and history of Buchanan's birthplace. You will also learn
about his rise to presidency, and his niece, Harriet Lane Johnston.

Link to this Internet site from http://www.myreportlinks.com

▶**Buchanan, James**
This Web site offers a brief overview of James Buchanan. Here you will learn
about his life, political career, and presidency. You will also find links to
information about the electoral process and presidential documents.

Link to this Internet site from http://www.myreportlinks.com

▶**Dred Scott's fight for freedom**
This PBS Web site tells the story behind the *Dred Scott* case and information
about the Supreme Court's decision.

Link to this Internet site from http://www.myreportlinks.com

Report Links

 The Internet sites described below can be accessed at
http://www.myreportlinks.com

▶**James Buchanan**
At this site you will find a brief overview of James Buchanan.
Here you will learn about his early life, political career, and his life
after retirement.

Link to this Internet site from http://www.myreportlinks.com

▶**James Buchanan**
This ThinkQuest Web site contains a brief biography of James
Buchanan. You will also find links to his inaugural address, a quote, an
interesting fact, and a list of the members of his administration.

Link to this Internet site from http://www.myreportlinks.com

▶**James Buchanan**
This is the place to find basic facts about James Buchanan. You will
learn about his family, youth, hobbies, and career.

Link to this Internet site from http://www.myreportlinks.com

▶**James Buchanan**
At this Web site you will find the biography of James Buchanan, the
results of his 1856 election, and his inaugural address.

Link to this Internet site from http://www.myreportlinks.com

▶**James Buchanan**
This brief biography of James Buchanan provides basic facts about his
life and presidency.

Link to this Internet site from http://www.myreportlinks.com

▶**James Buchanan**
A detailed account of the important events in Buchanan's political life
and presidential administration is given.

Link to this Internet site from http://www.myreportlinks.com

The Internet sites described below can be accessed at
http://www.myreportlinks.com

▶**James Buchanan (1791–1868)**
The National Portrait Galley holds paintings of each president.
View Buchanan's portrait and read a brief description about him and
the artist.

Link to this Internet site from http://www.myreportlinks.com

▶**James Buchanan Foundation**
At the official site of Wheatland, the home of James Buchanan, you will find
information about the mansion and the biographies of James Buchanan and
Harriet Lane Johnston.

Link to this Internet site from http://www.myreportlinks.com

▶**James Buchanan: Inaugural Address**
Bartleby.com provides the text of James Buchanan's inaugural address, which
was delivered on Wednesday, March 4, 1857.

Link to this Internet site from http://www.myreportlinks.com

▶**James Buchanan's Obituary**
At this Web site you will find the *New York Times* obituary of James
Buchanan, who died on June 1, 1868. Here you will learn how Buchanan's
administration and political career were viewed in his lifetime.

Link to this Internet site from http://www.myreportlinks.com

▶**Mr. President: Profiles of our Nation's Leaders**
This Web site provides a brief profile of James Buchanan where you will find
"fast facts" and a quote from Buchanan.

Link to this Internet site from http://www.myreportlinks.com

▶**On This Day: November 29, 1862**
At this Web site you can read an editorial from *Harper's Weekly* about former
President James Buchanan.

Link to this Internet site from http://www.myreportlinks.com

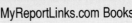

Report Links

➤ The Internet sites described below can be accessed at
http://www.myreportlinks.com

▶ **Presidents: James Buchanan**
At this Web site you will learn about James Buchanan's early years and presidency. You will also find lists of his cabinet, family members, major events in his term, and more.

Link to this Internet site from http://www.myreportlinks.com

▶ **Stephen A. Douglas Was Born**
America's Story from America's Library, a Library of Congress Web site describes Stephen A. Douglas's and President James Buchanan's opposing views with regards to United States expansion and slavery.

Link to this Internet site from http://www.myreportlinks.com

▶ **Today in History: The Little Giant**
At this Library of Congress Web site you will learn about James Buchanan's and Stephen A. Douglas's differing opinions about new territories and slavery. You will also find links to the Kansas-Nebraska Act and information about the Compromise of 1850.

Link to this Internet site from http://www.myreportlinks.com

▶ **The White House: Harriet Lane**
The official White House Web site holds the biography of Harriet Lane, James Buchanan's niece and White House hostess. Here you will learn about her life and experiences in the White House during Buchanan's administration.

Link to this Internet site from http://www.myreportlinks.com

▶ **The White House: James Buchanan**
The official White House Web site holds the biography of James Buchanan. Here you will learn about the difficulties Buchanan had uniting the country as the slavery issue became more prominent.

Link to this Internet site from http://www.myreportlinks.com

▶ **The White House Historical Association**
At the White House Historical Association you can explore the rich history of the White House and the presidents of the United States. You can also take a virtual tour of the White House, visit the president's park, and experience past presidential inaugurations.

Link to this Internet site from http://www.myreportlinks.com

Highlights

1791—*April 23:* James Buchanan is born in Cove Gap, Pennsylvania.

1807—Admitted to Dickinson College in Carlise, Pennsylvania.

1809—Graduates from Dickinson College.

1812—Admitted to the Pennsylvania Bar and begins practicing law in Lancaster, Pennsylvania.

1814–1815—Serves in the Pennsylvania House of Representatives.

1821–1831—Serves in the U.S. House of Representatives.

1832–1833—Serves as U.S. minister to Russia.

1834–1845—Serves in the U.S. Senate.

1845–1849—Serves as U.S. secretary of state.

1853–1856—Serves as U.S. minister to Great Britain.

1854—Co-authors Ostend Manifesto.

1856—Elected fifteenth president of the United States.

1857—*March 4:* Buchanan is inaugurated president.

—Sends troops to Utah Territory to stop rebellion led by Brigham Young.

1858—*May 11:* Minnesota is admitted as thirty-second state.

1859—Oregon admitted as thirty-third state.

1860—*Dec. 20:* South Carolina secedes from the Union.

1861—*Jan.–Feb.:* Mississippi, Florida, Alabama, Georgia, Louisiana, and Texas secede from the Union.

—*Jan. 29:* Kansas is admitted as thirty-fourth state.

—*March 4:* Retires to his estate in Lancaster, Pennsylvania, after the inauguration of President Lincoln.

1868—*June 1:* Dies at his Wheatland estate. The cause of death was pneumonia and an inflammation of the heart.

Under Investigation, 1859

President James Buchanan was angered and outraged. Congressman John Covode of Pennsylvania had introduced a resolution calling for a secret investigation of corruption in the Buchanan Administration. The resolution called for the appointment of a five-member committee to conduct the investigation starting in March 1859. If they found any evidence of official misconduct, then impeachment proceedings would follow.

Congressman Covode had a grudge against the president. Covode was a prominent member of a railroad company that wanted to acquire land in several western states. He got Congress to pass a bill which donated the land to his company. Covode hid this deal in a bill to establish agricultural colleges. On February 24, 1859, President Buchanan vetoed (refused to sign) the bill.

Covode was determined to ruin President Buchanan, but Buchanan fought back. On March 28, Buchanan protested to the House of Representatives. He denounced the secret investigation as politically motivated and told the members of the House that they were disgracing themselves by approving the investigation. He noted that his chief accuser, Congressman Covode, was also the committee's chairman.

"Mr. John Covode," Buchanan said, "is the accuser of the President . . . The House has made my accuser one of my judges . . . I defy all investigation. Nothing but the basest perjury can sully my good name."[1]

The House rejected the president's protest. The investigation continued until June. For witnesses, they sought out former government workers who had been dismissed by President Buchanan. The investigators found some practices which dated back to Andrew Jackson's administration. Government printing contracts went to newspaper editors who backed the party in power. That was nothing new.

The worst thing they found was that the postmaster of New York City had stolen $160,000 in federal funds and then fled to Europe to avoid arrest. They could not find a single impeachable offense against the president himself.

In a spirited reply to the House, President Buchanan pointedly asked them why they failed to recommend any articles of impeachment. He also rebuked the House for the gross unfairness of the proceedings. ". . . after proceeding for three months in secrecy without permitting any testimony on behalf of the accused, the committee had found nothing on which to ground a specific complaint." President Buchanan

President James Buchanan.

concluded by writing: "I have passed triumphantly through this ordeal. My vindication is complete."[2]

The victory over Covode's committee would be one the few pleasant memories James Buchanan would have of his troubled presidency. History would judge him harshly.

President Buchanan would be remembered as a weak leader who regarded slaves as private property and not as human beings and failed to keep the southern states from seceding (withdrawing) from the Union. This helped lead to the horrendous Civil War.

President James Buchanan was cleared of wrongdoing by the Covode Committe, but throughout history he has been judged harshly.

Chapter 2

Early Years, 1791–1812

James Buchanan was born in a log cabin at Cove Gap, Pennsylvania, on April 23, 1791. His father, James, Sr., was born in Ireland and emigrated to the United States in 1783. He was a prosperous merchant and farmer. James's mother, Elizabeth Speer Buchanan, was born in Greensburg, Pennsylvania. She married James, Sr., in 1788 when she was twenty-one, and he was twenty-seven.

James was the second of eleven children. As soon as he was tall enough to see over the counter, he began working in his father's store. James impressed customers by quickly and accurately totaling their bills without using paper and pencil. When talking to customers, he showed the self-assurance of a mature adult.

That behavior should have delighted James, Sr., but he seemed to be unimpressed. His father was generous with criticism and sparing with praise. They treated each other more like man-to-man business partners, than a playful, loving father and son.

▶ A Brilliant Scholar

Still, James occupied a special place in the family. As the firstborn son, he was expected to get the most education. James's sisters would learn to read and write, but that was secondary to knowing how to cook, clean, and sew. When he was old enough to start school, James was enrolled at the grammar school in Mercersburg, Pennsylvania. After finishing grammar school, James studied Latin and Greek at Old Stone Academy in Mercersburg. James did so well at Old Stone Academy that he was able to start college when he was only sixteen.

Troublemaker

In the fall of 1807, James was enrolled as a junior at Dickinson College in Carlisle, Pennsylvania. James studied hard, but he also played hard. That got him into trouble. What exactly he did is not known. It is known that James took to drinking, smoking, and sometimes staying out late.

After completing his first year of college, James returned home for a vacation. He was sitting in the parlor with his father when a letter arrived for James, Sr. It was from the school. James anxiously watched his father read the letter. He saw that his father was upset. James, Sr., handed the letter to his son and then left without saying anything.

The letter was signed by Dr. Robert Davidson, the president of Dickinson College. It said that James was being expelled. It also said that if he had not been the son of the well-respected James Buchanan, Sr., James would have been expelled earlier. Dr. Davidson added that Dickinson College did not want James to return there "under any circumstances."[1]

James could not face his father. He went to Dr. John King who was a well-known pastor and a Dickinson College trustee. Dr. King told James that he would get him back in school only if he would solemnly promise to change his ways. James readily agreed.

A New Attitude

James returned to Dickinson with a very different attitude. He was still tempted to play around, but he held fast to his pledge. He attended all his classes, studied hard, and did

well on all his tests. James had excelled scholastically and he expected to be honored for his hard work. Instead, the college rebuffed him. The faculty decided they should not honor a student with James's reputation. They felt that he had been a troublemaker and had been disrespectful to them.

James was furious. He believed that he should receive scholastic honors, because no one had better grades than his. He thought about skipping the graduation ceremonies. Eventually he changed his mind. James attended commencement, but he left Dickinson College "feeling but little attachment for the Alma Mater."[2]

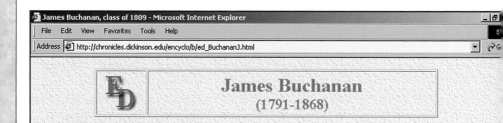

James Buchanan, class of 1809 - Microsoft Internet Explorer

File   Edit   View   Favorites   Tools   Help

Address http://chronicles.dickinson.edu/encyclo/b/ed_BuchananJ.html

James Buchanan
(1791-1868)

James Buchanan, fifteenth president of the United States, was born near Mercersburg, Pennsylvania on April 23, 1791 to parents of Scotch-Irish descent. Buchanan attended the Mercersburg Academy until the fall of 1807, when he entered the junior class of Dickinson College.

He found the school to be in "wretched condition" with "no efficient discipline." However, his own behavior while at Dickinson was far from exemplary; he was expelled during the fall vacation of 1808 for bad behavior. After making a pledge of good behavior to his minister, Dr. John King (a college trustee), Buchanan was readmitted to Dickinson. In his senior year, he felt slighted by the faculty because he did not win the top award of the College for which his literary society had nominated him. Buchanan commented, "I left college, . . . feeling little attachment to the Alma Mater."

Upon graduation, Buchanan began to study under the prominent Lancaster lawyer James Hopkins. After being admitted to the Pennsylvania Bar in 1812, he quickly gained prominence, and was elected to the Pennsylvania House of Representatives in 1814 and 1815 as a Federalist. Thus began Buchanan's long career as a public

Done   Internet

James Buchanan attended Dickinson College from 1807 until 1809.

▶ Preparing for the Future

After graduation, James Buchanan returned to his parents house in Mercersburg for some rest and relaxation. He spent about two months hunting and helping his father out in the store and around the farm. James, Jr., thought about his future and what profession he would enter.

By December, James Buchanan, Jr., made up his mind. He wanted to be a lawyer. James, Sr., made the arrangements. James, Jr., began studying law by clerking in the office of James Hopkins in Lancaster, Pennsylvania.

At that time, Lancaster was the capital of Pennsylvania. It was a bustling town with many taverns and other diversions. Buchanan was often tempted to shirk his studies, but he steadfastly applied himself to learning the law.

". . . I studied law, and nothing but law."[3] Buchanan would recall. Even when relaxing, he would think about his studies. While watching a sunset, he would think about what he had read and work at putting the material into words.

In November 1812, Buchanan became a lawyer. He opened an office in Lancaster. There were few clients and much competition. At first, he had a hard time making a living.

Buchanan began to think about going into politics. Before he was able to run for office, war intervened. In June 1812, Congress voted to declare war on England. At that time, Buchanan belonged to the Federalist Party. Most Federalists were opposed to the War of 1812. Buchanan's opposition changed to support when the British burned Washington, D.C., and began marching on Baltimore.

At a meeting in Lancaster in 1814, Buchanan gave his first public speech. Stirred by patriotic fervor, he volunteered to fight the British and urged others to join

him. Two days later, Buchanan rode with a company of dragoons (soldiers on horseback) headed for Baltimore.

James Buchanan and his fellow volunteers never saw battle. After arriving in Baltimore, they received orders to go outside the city and acquire horses for the army. By the time they completed their mission, the British had withdrawn from Baltimore. A few weeks later, the volunteers were sent home.

▲ As a member of the Federalist Party, Buchanan strongly opposed the War of 1812. This changed when the British burned the Capitol and the White House on August 24, 1814.

First Political Office

Shortly after returning to Lancaster, Buchanan was elected to the state legislature. His joy at being elected was brought down by his father's lack of excitement for him. Instead of sending congratulations, James, Sr., wrote: "Perhaps your going to the Legislature may be to your advantage & it may be otherwise, I hope that you will make the best of the thing now . . ."[4]

James would heed his father's advice and make the best of the situation. One office would lead to another and put James Buchanan on the path to the presidency. For the next fifty years, Buchanan would be immersed in politics.

Young Politician, 1815–1821

James spent his first weeks in the legislature listening, looking, and learning. That was how new lawmakers were expected to act. He carefully observed which colleagues were eloquent and forceful speakers and which were dull and boring. During speeches and debates, he watched how other legislators reacted to phrases, gestures, and arguments. James decided he would not make a speech without thoroughly rehearsing it.

▶ Philosophical Differences

His first speech was during a debate on drafting soldiers. The War of 1812 was still raging, and there were rumors that the British were poised to launch an attack on Philadelphia. Buchanan argued that the army should be all volunteers instead of draftees. He felt that wealthier people would be less likely to be drafted. That displeased some of his fellow Federalists. One of his Federalist colleagues even told Buchanan he should leave the party to become a Democrat. A few years later, he would.

▶ Helped By His Looks

In 1815, Buchanan was reelected to the legislature. His speaking talents and pleasing physical appearance helped him win votes. He was just over six feet tall with broad shoulders, wavy blond hair, and large blue eyes. His most noticeable characteristic was the way he tilted his head forward and sideways when speaking or listening to someone.

Buchanan tilted his head because of a vision defect. He was nearsighted in one eye and farsighted in the other. His tilted head gave people the impression that he was particularly shy and humble.

The highlight of Buchanan's second term in the legislature was his opposition to efforts to recharter the Bank of the United States. The bank's charter had expired before the War of 1812. By 1815, many Americans had lost faith in the paper currency issued by the U.S. Treasury. Gold coins and bartering (trading goods and services for other goods and services) had largely replaced paper currency.

Once again, Buchanan was at odds with members of his party. He sided with President James Madison. They both believed that a strong central bank put too much control into the hands of a few. Congress rechartered the bank in 1816, but Buchanan continued to wonder if he was out of step with his party.

Buchanan did not seek reelection to a third term in the legislature. It was customary then to only serve two terms, but he probably wanted to leave. His law practice was becoming more lucrative and taking up more of his time. Leaving the legislature also gave him time to pursue the one great romance of his life.

▶ A Shattered Romance

In 1819, Buchanan began dating Ann Coleman. Her father, Robert Coleman, was a millionaire iron mill owner who distrusted Buchanan. He thought Buchanan was more interested in the family fortune than Ann's love and affection. In spite of his misgivings, Buchanan and Ann Coleman became engaged.

Ann abruptly ended their engagement when she learned that Buchanan had casually visited another woman.

Apparently, Buchanan had no romantic interest in the other woman. Still, Ann refused to listen to his side. Letters Buchanan wrote to her were returned unopened.

In December 1819, Ann Coleman left her home in Lancaster to visit some relatives in Philadelphia. Five days later, she died. It is believed she overdosed on some medicine. There were also rumors of suicide, but it was never proven.

Buchanan wrote Robert Coleman and asked permission to see Ann before her burial and to attend her funeral. Buchanan wrote: ". . . I may sustain the shock of her death, but I feel that happiness has fled from me forever."[1] The letter was returned unopened.

Buchanan was shattered. He left his Lancaster law office without telling anyone where he was going. He went to Mercersburg for solace and sympathy from his mother and father. He neglected his law practice. After spending Christmas with his family, he was ready to face life without Ann.

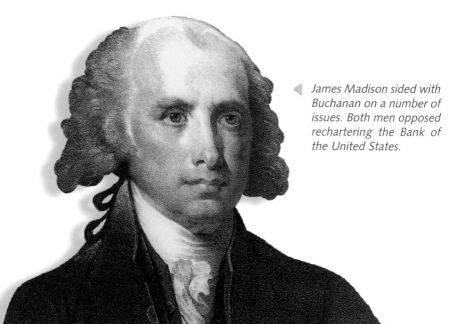

James Madison sided with Buchanan on a number of issues. Both men opposed rechartering the Bank of the United States.

James Buchanan would never have another serious romantic relationship. To this day, he remains America's only bachelor president.

Congressman Buchanan

James thought about leaving Lancaster. Politics provided him with the opportunity. In the spring of 1820, some Federalist Party leaders asked him to be their candidate for Congress. James agreed. In October 1820, Buchanan was elected to the U.S. House of Representatives.

Before going to Washington, James had to settle his father's estate. James, Sr., had died in June 1821 without leaving a will. James spent the remainder of the summer working on the complicated legal matter. He worked out a settlement which provided financial security for his mother, paid for the education of three brothers, and provided for his two unmarried sisters.

Then, in December 1821, Buchanan was sworn in as a member of the seventeenth Congress.

Chapter 4

Congressman and Diplomat, 1821–1834

For the next ten years, Buchanan would devote himself to being an effective congressman. He entered Congress at a time when the influence of the Federalist Party was waning. In the 1820 presidential election, the immensely popular President James Monroe had run unopposed.

▶ Small Beginnings

Monroe's party, the Democratic-Republicans, was the forerunner of today's Democratic Party. In the seventeenth Congress, the Democratic-Republicans held 44 of the 48 seats in the Senate and 158 of the 183 seats in the House.

Buchanan knew that as first-term congressman in a minority party, he would not have much power. He kept in touch with the voters in his district and did his best to represent their interests. Buchanan strongly supported high tariffs (taxes) on imported goods. High tariffs kept imports from being sold at a lower price than similar goods manufactured in his district.

Buchanan also supported public education and continued to oppose the national bank. He passionately

President James Monroe.

believed that rich and poor should be treated equally. He usually supported the rights of individual states over the power of the federal government.

Growing Influence

Buchanan was reelected to the House of Representatives four times. As he gained seniority, he gained influence and became known as a behind-the-scenes politician who could make deals and sway votes. Although he was elected as a Federalist, Buchanan continued to distance himself from the party. In 1824, he supported Andrew Jackson's unsuccessful bid for the presidency.

After Jackson was defeated by John Quincy Adams, Buchanan became a leading opponent of the Adams Administration. In 1822, Buchanan had supported the extension of a major highway known as the Cumberland Road. When President Adams proposed extending it, Buchanan opposed it, but the road was extended anyway. Buchanan also helped to prevent President Adams from sending American representatives to the Panama Congress of 1828.

Position on Slavery

During the Quincy Adams Administration, Buchanan also made his first public pronouncements on slavery. Buchanan denounced slavery as "a great political and a great moral evil," but he also called it "an evil at present without a remedy." He even said that abolishing slavery would just make things worse.

Apparently Buchanan believed that if slaves were emancipated (freed) they would rise up and kill their former masters. He rhetorically asked: "Is there any man in this union who could, for a moment, indulge in the

horrible idea of abolishing slavery by the massacre of the high-minded and chivalrous race of men in the South? I trust there is not one."[1]

▶ A Change in Party

In 1828, the Democrats nominated Jackson to run against President Adams. Buchanan no longer called himself a Federalist. He ran for reelection as a Democrat and actively campaigned for Jackson. His support helped Jackson win the state of Pennsylvania and the presidential election.

Buchanan was rewarded for his support. His brother George was appointed district attorney for the Pittsburgh region. As a Democrat, Buchanan was a member of the majority party. He became the chairman of the House Judiciary Committee. He had the chance to become an influential and important congressional leader in the Jackson Administration. Yet, in 1830, Buchanan left politics to return to his law practice in Lancaster.

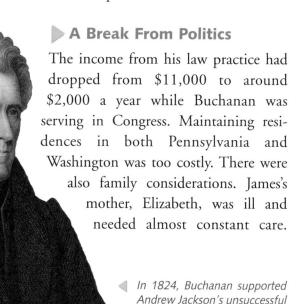

▶ A Break From Politics

The income from his law practice had dropped from $11,000 to around $2,000 a year while Buchanan was serving in Congress. Maintaining residences in both Pennsylvania and Washington was too costly. There were also family considerations. James's mother, Elizabeth, was ill and needed almost constant care.

◀ *In 1824, Buchanan supported Andrew Jackson's unsuccessful bid for the presidency.*

Rebuilding his law practice became more important than staying in Congress.

Buchanan, however, was not able to stay away from politics and public service for long. Less than three months after leaving Congress, he was secretly offered the position of U.S. minister to Russia. He was flattered, but he had some serious reservations about accepting the post. However, President Jackson was persistent and persuasive. Buchanan finally agreed to return to public service.

▶ Minister to Russia

In January 1832, the Senate confirmed Buchanan's appointment. He left for Russia in April 1832 and arrived at his post in St. Petersburg in June. He did his best to get a commercial trading agreement between the United States and Russia. The Jackson Administration also wanted him to negotiate maritime rights for American ships in Russian waters.

President John ▶ Quincy Adams.

▶ Return to Washington

Buchanan was able to get a trade agreement signed. Realizing, though, that a maritime agreement was not to be, Buchanan asked to be replaced. In the spring of 1833, President Jackson gave him permission to return home. Senator William Wilkins of Pennsylvania was chosen to replace Buchanan. That created a vacancy in the U.S. Senate. At that time, senators were elected by state legislatures instead of direct popular vote.

After being approached by some party leaders, Buchanan agreed to run for the Senate. He won out over three other candidates. In December 1834, Buchanan took his seat in the Senate. He was back in Washington, and he would stay there for the next fifteen years.

Chapter 5

Senator to Presidential Candidate, 1836–1856

After returning to Washington, Buchanan remained a staunch supporter of the Jackson Administration. In 1836, President Jackson declined to seek a third term. He designated Vice President Martin Van Buren to be his successor. Buchanan quickly aligned himself with Van Buren and actively campaigned for him.

After Van Buren was elected president, the Pennsylvania Legislature reelected Buchanan to the Senate. The Democrats now held the presidency and were the majority party in both houses of Congress. Buchanan would not face reelection for another six years. Assuming that Van Buren served two terms, Buchanan could campaign for the presidency in 1844.

▶ An Intense Debate

During Buchanan's time in the Senate, the debate over slavery became more heated and more persistent. His position was well known. He detested slavery and denounced it as an evil institution. However, he believed there was no way to eliminate it. He viewed slavery as a legal and constitutional issue instead of a moral issue.

Buchanan looked at slaves as being private property instead of citizens. He took the position that the federal government could not interfere with the property rights of a slaveholder. Buchanan also blamed abolitionists (people who wanted to abolish slavery) for the nation's problems.[1]

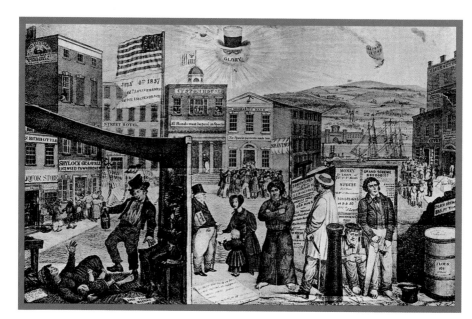

▲ The Panic of 1837 caused many banks to close, affecting everyone from the prosperous merchant to the humblest laborer.

▶ Panic of 1837

About two months after Van Buren was inaugurated, a major economic crisis followed. It came to be known as the Panic of 1837. Many banks were freely investing in the sale of public lands. They were lax about loaning money to land speculators. Shortly before leaving office, President Jackson issued an order stating that buyers of public lands had to pay in gold or silver. Banks were unable to make loans and many went out of business. Soon, there was rising unemployment, and America suffered its first major economic depression.

▶ A Bump in the Road

The Panic of 1837 doomed Van Buren to be a one-term president. In 1840, Van Buren was defeated for reelection by the Whig candidate, William Henry Harrison. The Democrats suffered other losses. The Whigs gained control of the House and the Senate. If Buchanan had been up for reelection in 1840, it is likely that he would have lost.

President Harrison unexpectedly died after one month in office. He was succeeded by Vice President John Tyler. President Tyler split with the Whigs when he vetoed a bill to reestablish the National Bank. His party then refused to nominate him for a second term.

In 1844, the Democrats nominated James K. Polk of Tennessee as their presidential candidate. Buchanan fully supported Polk. He campaigned hard for Polk while seeking a third term in the Senate. Both men were elected.

▷ Secretary of State

James Buchanan made plans for returning to the Senate. He had become chairman of the Foreign Relations Committee, and he looked forward to leading that important committee. Yet, he wondered if Polk might be considering him for a position in his cabinet.

On February 17, 1845, Buchanan received a letter from the president-elect asking him to serve as his secretary of state. The offer was made with one important condition. If he decided to run for president in 1848, Buchanan would have to resign from the cabinet. Polk wanted all of his cabinet members to be devoted to serving his administration, not to furthering their political careers.

Buchanan answered Polk by writing: "I cannot proclaim to the world that in no contingency shall I be a candidate in 1848 . . ."[2] He made his position clear; he would not rule out a run for the presidency to serve in Polk's cabinet. The president-elect apparently respected his

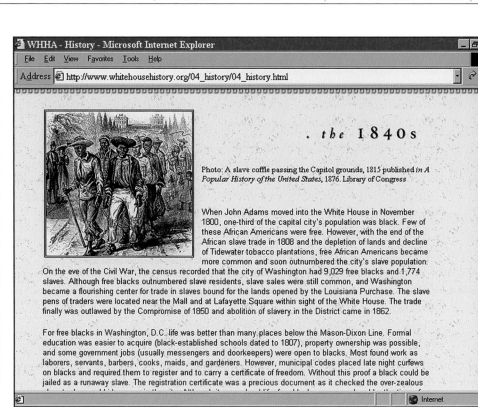

WHHA - History - Microsoft Internet Explorer

File   Edit   View   Favorites   Tools   Help

Address http://www.whitehousehistory.org/04_history/04_history.html

. the 1840s

Photo: A slave coffle passing the Capitol grounds, 1815 published *in A Popular History of the United States*, 1876. Library of Congress

When John Adams moved into the White House in November 1800, one-third of the capital city's population was black. Few of these African Americans were free. However, with the end of the African slave trade in 1808 and the depletion of lands and decline of Tidewater tobacco plantations, free African Americans became more common and soon outnumbered the city's slave population. On the eve of the Civil War, the census recorded that the city of Washington had 9,029 free blacks and 1,774 slaves. Although free blacks outnumbered slave residents, slave sales were still common, and Washington became a flourishing center for trade in slaves bound for the lands opened by the Louisiana Purchase. The slave pens of traders were located near the Mall and at Lafayette Square within sight of the White House. The trade finally was outlawed by the Compromise of 1850 and abolition of slavery in the District came in 1862.

For free blacks in Washington, D.C. life was better than many places below the Mason-Dixon Line. Formal education was easier to acquire (black-established schools dated to 1807), property ownership was possible, and some government jobs (usually messengers and doorkeepers) were open to blacks. Most found work as laborers, servants, barbers, cooks, maids, and gardeners. However, municipal codes placed late night curfews on blacks and required them to register and to carry a certificate of freedom. Without this proof a black could be jailed as a runaway slave. The registration certificate was a precious document as it checked the over-zealous

Internet

▲ *Buchanan supported the institution of slavery, believing that the U.S. Constitution allowed it. He often avoided the issue, declaring that laws could not change the morals of society.*

honesty and plainspoken nature. James Buchanan became Polk's secretary of state.

▶ Conflict

Serving as secretary of state enhanced Buchanan's political resume, but it came at a cost. President Polk was outspoken about his foreign policy goals. He preferred to work quietly, slowly, and behind the scenes. Polk would often act as his own secretary of state. At times, the two politicians were competing instead of working together.

Still, significant achievements were made. A border dispute between the United States and Britain over the Oregon Territory was settled. Texas was annexed and joined the Union as the twenty-eighth state. The Treaty of Guadalupe Hidalgo, which ended the Mexican War, settled the border between the United States and Mexico and allowed the United States to acquire more than 500,000 square miles of new territory.

Two Runs for the Presidency

In 1848, Buchanan decided to make a full-fledged run for the presidency. However, he finished a distant second to Lewis Cass of Michigan for the Democratic Party nomination. Zachary Taylor defeated Cass in the presidential election.

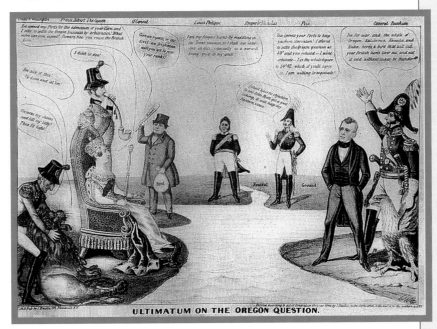

This political cartoon illustrates the Oregon Question, one of the first major issues that President Polk had to face. The Queen of England (seated in her throne) and Polk (second from the right) argued over the northern border of the Oregon Territory.

Buchanan left Washington and returned to his law practice in Lancaster. In 1852, he made another run for the White House. For ten ballots, Buchanan was the leading candidate at the Democratic National Convention. After forty-nine ballots, though, the nomination went to Franklin Pierce of New Hampshire.

James Buchanan worked to get Pierce elected. Pierce rewarded him by naming him the U.S. minister to Great Britain. He negotiated some commercial trade agreements between the two nations, but he is most remembered for his support of the Ostend Manifesto.

▶ The Ostend Manifesto

The Ostend Manifesto was drawn up by Buchanan and the U.S. ministers to Spain and France. The document stated that if Spain refused to sell Cuba to the United States, the island could be acquired by any means necessary. President Pierce formally condemned the Ostend Manifesto, but it boosted Buchanan's popularity in the South. Southern leaders eyed Cuba as fertile ground for the expansion of slavery.

In the spring of 1856, Buchanan announced his intention to leave his diplomatic post and return to the United States. Buchanan returned to Lancaster and began campaigning for the Democratic presidential nomination.

▶ A Reoccurring Theme

The dominant political issue was slavery. President Pierce had supported the Kansas-Nebraska Act. The act said that the settlers of the Kansas and Nebraska Territories, not Congress, would vote to decide if they would join the Union as free states or as slave states. This was known as *popular sovereignty.*

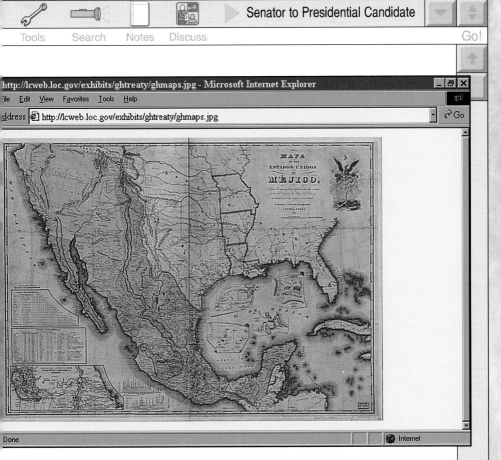

http://lcweb.loc.gov/exhibits/ghtreaty/ghmaps.jpg - Microsoft Internet Explorer

File   Edit   View   Favorites   Tools   Help

Address   http://lcweb.loc.gov/exhibits/ghtreaty/ghmaps.jpg   Go

Done   Internet

This map shows the territory that United States gained as a result of the Treaty of Guadalupe Hidalgo. Much of the Southwestern United States was carved out of this land.

The unexpected result was a virtual civil war in Kansas. Pro-slavery and antislavery forces battled to settle the territory and seize political power. Over two hundred people were killed in the struggle known as Bleeding Kansas. Since he was in England while this occurred, Buchanan's position on the Kansas-Nebraska Act was not known. This would work to his advantage when the Democrats chose their presidential nominee.

Chapter 6

President Buchanan, 1856–1861

When the Democrats began their 1856 national convention, Buchanan was the leading candidate for the presidential nomination. His two major opponents, President Pierce and Senator Stephen Douglas, were hurt by their support of the Kansas-Nebraska Act. Buchanan was not damaged by the slavery issue, and his support of the Ostend Manifesto gained him the backing of Southern delegates.

After twelve ballots, President Pierce was out of the running. After sixteen ballots, Senator Douglas withdrew. On the seventeenth ballot, James Buchanan became the

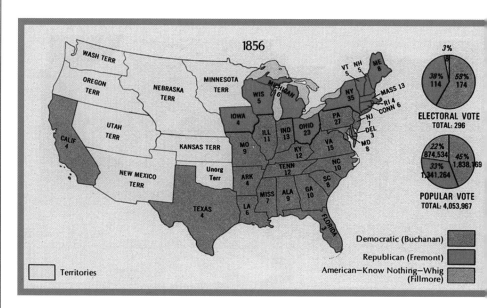

▲ This map shows the results of the presidential election of 1856.

Party's unanimous choice. John C. Breckinridge of Kentucky was nominated to be his vice president.

The Election of 1856

The 1856 presidential election was a three-man race. The newly-formed Republican Party chose famed explorer John C. Fremont as their presidential candidate. The American Party (also nicknamed the Know-Nothing Party because party members would say: "I know nothing" when asked about their political party) nominated former President Millard Fillmore.

The Republicans attracted abolitionists and other anti-slavery elements. The American Party favored limiting all public offices to native-born, non-Catholic citizens. The Democrats had the support of southerners and pro-slavery voters. Buchanan also drew support from voters who believed in a strict interpretation of the constitution.

Since there were three candidates, Buchanan got less than 50 percent of the popular vote. He received 1,838,169 votes to 1,335,264 for Fremont, and 874,534 for Fillmore. Buchanan won the electoral votes of nineteen states for a total of 174 electoral votes compared to 114 for Fremont and 8 for Fillmore. After spending over forty years in politics, sixty-five-year-old James Buchanan was elected president of the United States.

On March 4, 1857, President James Buchanan was inaugurated. In his inaugural address, he said little about slavery. He talked of how the country was in sound financial shape and announced his intentions to purchase Cuba and Alaska. Once again, he spoke of slavery as a legal issue and naively said: "May we not, then, hope that the long agitation on this subject is approaching its end . . ."[1]

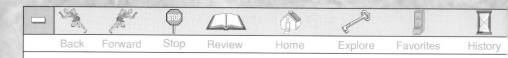

Back   Forward   Stop   Review   Home   Explore   Favorites   History

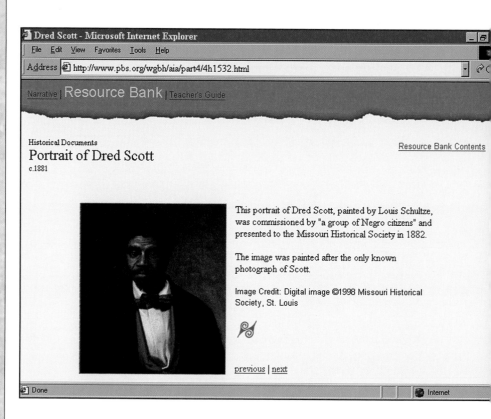

Dred Scott - Microsoft Internet Explorer

File   Edit   View   Favorites   Tools   Help

Address   http://www.pbs.org/wgbh/aia/part4/4h1532.html

Narrative | Resource Bank | Teacher's Guide

Historical Documents

Portrait of Dred Scott

c.1881

Resource Bank Contents

This portrait of Dred Scott, painted by Louis Schultze, was commissioned by "a group of Negro citizens" and presented to the Missouri Historical Society in 1882.

The image was painted after the only known photograph of Scott.

Image Credit: Digital image ©1998 Missouri Historical Society, St. Louis

previous | next

Done   Internet

▲ The Supreme Court handed down the controversial Dred Scott decision in 1857. Dred Scott, pictured here, was a slave who sued for his freedom.

▶ *Dred Scott*

Shortly after Buchanan was sworn in as president, the Supreme Court handed down the controversial *Dred Scott* decision. Scott was a slave who had been taken by his master from the slave state of Missouri into the free state of Illinois and the Wisconsin Territory. After returning to Missouri, Scott sued for his freedom. He argued that being a temporary resident of a free state and a free territory, made him a free man.

By a 7 to 2 majority, the Supreme Court ruled that because Scott was a slave, he was property and not a United States citizen. Therefore, he had no right to sue. Buchanan strongly supported the decision and hoped it would end the slavery issue, but it simply made things worse.

By a smaller majority, the Supreme Court also ruled that since slaves were property, Congress had no legal authority to forbid slavery in the territories. To do so, the Court reasoned, would violate a slaveholder's constitutional right to own property.

Kansas Territory

Another issue President Buchanan had to deal with immediately was the situation in the Kansas Territory. Buchanan appointed Robert J. Walker of Mississippi to serve as the territorial governor. While Walker was governor, a state constitutional convention was held in Lecompton, Kansas. The convention was boycotted by the antislavery forces. The result was a constitution which called for the admission of Kansas as a slave state.

Buchanan supported the pro-slavery constitution and asked Congress to approve it. Senator Stephen Douglas led the fight against its adoption. He argued that Kansas voters were denied a chance to vote for it. In 1858, the voters of Kansas rejected the constitution. Buchanan still fought for its approval. Congress ordered a second election, but the result was the same. Finally, Kansas entered the Union as a free state in January 1861.

A Financial Panic

The Buchanan Administration was also marred by a financial panic in 1857. In August of that year, the Ohio

Stephen A. Douglas Was Born - Microsoft Internet Explorer

File Edit View Favorites Tools Help

Address http://www.americaslibrary.gov/pages/jb_0423_litgiant_1_e.html

Internet

▲ *Stephen A. Douglas, nicknamed the "Little Giant," supported popular sovereignty, or the belief that territories should decide for themselves whether they wanted slavery.*

Life Insurance Company of Cincinnati suffered a financial collapse. Soon, many banks were collapsing because people panicked and took out their money. The economic crisis was also heightened by a drop in the price of gold, reduced foreign demand for United States agricultural products, and rising unemployment.

Rather then directly aid the people affected, Buchanan proposed changing some banking laws. He felt bad for the people affected but gave them no financial assistance.

Democratic Setback

Buchanan's support of the *Dred Scott* decision and his stubbornness over the Kansas elections, hurt the Democrats in the 1858 midterm elections. The Republicans gained six seats in the Senate and twenty-two in the House of Representatives. That virtually insured the Democrats would pass no meaningful laws during Buchanan's final two years as president.

Foreign Policy Success

The Buchanan Administration did enjoy a few successes in foreign policy, but they were overshadowed by the domestic issues of slavery and secession. Commercial treaties with China and Japan were signed. Buchanan used his skills at diplomacy to get Great Britain to give up its land claims in Central America. The country of Paraguay violated a treaty by firing on an American ship and seizing property held by Americans. Buchanan sent a fleet of warships as a show of force, and Paraguay quickly backed off.

White House Social Life

Although he was a bachelor, Buchanan had some family in the White House. Buchanan's sister, Jane Lane, died when her daughter Harriet was a young girl, and Harriet chose to live with her Uncle James. Buchanan became her guardian when she was twelve, raised her, and paid for her education. Due to the fact that Buchanan was never married, Lane served as White House hostess during his time in office. With Buchanan and Lane in charge of social events, "White House entertainments took on a festive note."[2]

Back   Forward   Stop   Review   Home   Explore   Favorites   History

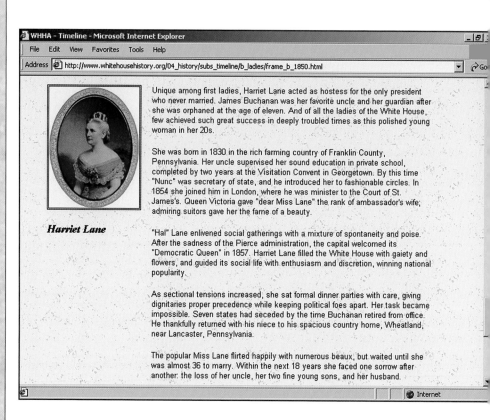

Unique among first ladies, Harriet Lane acted as hostess for the only president who never married. James Buchanan was her favorite uncle and her guardian after she was orphaned at the age of eleven. And of all the ladies of the White House, few achieved such great success in deeply troubled times as this polished young woman in her 20s.

She was born in 1830 in the rich farming country of Franklin County, Pennsylvania. Her uncle supervised her sound education in private school, completed by two years at the Visitation Convent in Georgetown. By this time "Nunc" was secretary of state, and he introduced her to fashionable circles. In 1854 she joined him in London, where he was minister to the Court of St. James's. Queen Victoria gave "dear Miss Lane" the rank of ambassador's wife; admiring suitors gave her the fame of a beauty.

Harriet Lane

"Hal" Lane enlivened social gatherings with a mixture of spontaneity and poise. After the sadness of the Pierce administration, the capital welcomed its "Democratic Queen" in 1857. Harriet Lane filled the White House with gaiety and flowers, and guided its social life with enthusiasm and discretion, winning national popularity.

As sectional tensions increased, she sat formal dinner parties with care, giving dignitaries proper precedence while keeping political foes apart. Her task became impossible. Seven states had seceded by the time Buchanan retired from office. He thankfully returned with his niece to his spacious country home, Wheatland, near Lancaster, Pennsylvania.

The popular Miss Lane flirted happily with numerous beaux, but waited until she was almost 36 to marry. Within the next 18 years she faced one sorrow after another: the loss of her uncle, her two fine young sons, and her husband.

Internet

Harriet Lane Johnston acted as White House hostess for her uncle and guardian, James Buchanan.

The End of His Political Career

Buchanan had wisely decided to only serve one term. By 1860, the Democrats were badly divided. They could not agree so they ran two candidates against the Republican nominee, Abraham Lincoln. After the Democrats nominated Senator Douglas, the Southern Democrats bolted the convention. They reassembled and nominated Vice President John C. Breckinridge of Kentucky as their candidate.

About six weeks after Lincoln was elected, South Carolina seceded from the Union. Before Buchanan left office, six other states seceded and formed the Confederate States of America. Buchanan took the position that secession was illegal, but the federal government had no constitutional authority to force a state to stay in the Union.[3]

Buchanan was widely ridiculed for the contradiction in his thinking—a state cannot legally secede, but the federal government cannot legally stop it. He would assert the authority of the federal government only to protect federal property. Buchanan was forced to do that when the Confederates demanded the surrender of Fort Sumter. The fort was located in the harbor of Charleston, South Carolina. Buchanan tried to send troops and supplies there in an unarmed steamship. The ship was forced to retreat after the Confederates fired upon it. This was clearly an act of war, but there was no motion in Congress for a declaration of war.

Even if Congress had declared war, the Union only had a few hundred troops at its disposal. Buchanan asked Congress to pass a Constitutional amendment guaranteeing slavery in the states that wanted it. His request was largely ignored. They had little interest in the wishes of a lame-duck (one who is leaving office) president.

Return to Lancaster

On March 4, 1861, Abraham Lincoln was inaugurated as America's sixteenth president. The outgoing and the incoming chief executives rode together in an open air carriage. During the ride, Buchanan turned to Lincoln and said: "My dear sir, if you are as happy in entering the White House as I shall feel on returning to Wheatland (his home in Lancaster), you are a happy man indeed."[4]

Chapter 7 ▶

A Quiet Retirement, 1861–1868

Buchanan returned to Lancaster to enjoy a hero's welcome. He was greeted with a thirty-four-gun presidential salute, a cheering crowd, and ringing church bells. There was a two-mile parade from the train station to the town square. A round of speeches followed. There was a band to greet him when he finally arrived at his Wheatland estate. It was both flattering and embarrassing.

▶ Fleeting Popularity

Once he settled back into his old home, Buchanan kept a low profile. He avidly read newspapers and wrote letters. He knew the Civil War was inevitable. When it broke out, he listened to critics in both parties blame him for failing to stop it.

As war casualties mounted, Buchanan received letters from people in the North and South alike. Mothers, fathers, and widows would write about their sons and husbands dying on battlefields and ask Buchanan why he did not stop the war from occurring. Buchanan defended himself by writing a book, *Mr. Buchanan's Administration*, on the eve of the rebellion. It was published in 1866, but it did little to change the public's opinion of him.

In May 1868, Buchanan was seriously ill from a cold and the complications of old age. He revised his will and made funeral and burial plans. On June 1, 1868, James Buchanan died at his Wheatland estate at the age of seventy-seven.

A Tainted Reputation

History has been harsh to James Buchanan. A 1962 historian's poll ranked him twenty-ninth of the thirty-one presidents they rated. He was at the bottom of the below average category.[1] He tried to please and appease both the North and South; pro-slavery and antislavery forces. He ended up pleasing hardly anyone. Buchanan failed to stop secession, but it is doubtful that any president with a hostile Congress and a weak military could have.

At another time, Buchanan might have been an effective president. He was a man of high character, intelligence, and patriotism. His poor performance as president helps us to realize how difficult the job is.

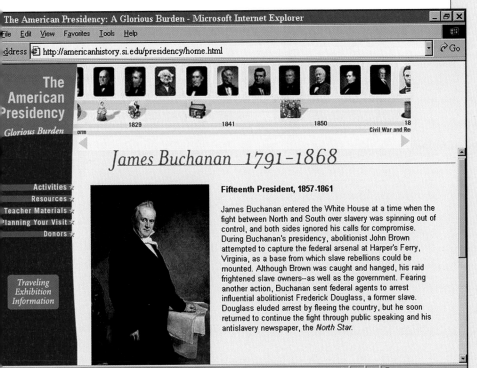

The American Presidency: A Glorious Burden - Microsoft Internet Explorer

File Edit View Favorites Tools Help

Address http://americanhistory.si.edu/presidency/home.html

The American Presidency

Glorious Burden

1829   1841   1850   18
Civil War and Re

James Buchanan 1791–1868

Activities
Resources
Teacher Materials
Planning Your Visit
Donors

Traveling Exhibition Information

Fifteenth President, 1857-1861

James Buchanan entered the White House at a time when the fight between North and South over slavery was spinning out of control, and both sides ignored his calls for compromise. During Buchanan's presidency, abolitionist John Brown attempted to capture the federal arsenal at Harper's Ferry, Virginia, as a base from which slave rebellions could be mounted. Although Brown was caught and hanged, his raid frightened slave owners--as well as the government. Fearing another action, Buchanan sent federal agents to arrest influential abolitionist Frederick Douglass, a former slave. Douglass eluded arrest by fleeing the country, but he soon returned to continue the fight through public speaking and his antislavery newspaper, the *North Star*.

Internet

President James Buchanan's administration was plagued by tensions between the North and South, which resulted in the Civil War.

Chapter 1. Under Investigation, 1859

1. Phillip S. Klein, *President James Buchanan A Biography* (University Park, Pa.: Pennsylvania State University, 1962), p. 338.

2. Ibid., pp. 339–340.

Chapter 2. Early Years, 1791–1812

1. Phillip S. Klein, *President James Buchanan: A Biography* (University Park, Pa.: Pennsylvania State University, 1962), p 10.

2. Ibid., p. 12.

3. Ibid., p. 14.

4. Ibid., p. 18.

Chapter 3. Young Politician, 1815–1821

1. Phillip S. Klein, *President James Buchanan A Biography* (University Park, Pa.: Pennsylvania State University, 1962), p. 32.

Chapter 4. Congressman and Diplomat, 1821–1834

1. Edwin P. Hoyt, *James Buchanan* (Chicago: Reilly & Lee, 1966), p. 23.

Chapter 5. Senator to Presidential Candidate, 1836–1856

1. Paul F. Boller, *Presidential Anecdotes* (New York: Oxford University Press, 1981), p. 119.

2. Edwin P. Hoyt, *James Buchanan* (Chicago: Reilly & Lee, 1966), p. 65.

Chapter 6. President Buchanan, 1856–1861

1. Philip S. Klein, *President James Buchanan: A Biography* (University Park, Pa.: Pennsylvania State University, 1962), p. 402.

2. Paul F. Boller, *Presidential Anecdotes* (New York: Oxford University Press, 1981), p. 119.

3. Ibid., p. 120.

4. William A. DeGregorio, *The Complete Book of U.S. Presidents* (New York: Dembner Books, 1984), p. 222.

Chapter 7. A Quiet Retirement, 1861–1868

1. William A DeGregorio, *The Complete Book of U.S. Presidents* (New York: Dembner Books, 1984), p. 221.

Further Reading

Birkner, Michael J. ed. *James Buchanan & the Political Crisis of the 1850s.* Cranbury, N.J.: Susquehanna University Press, 1996.

Brill, Marlene T. *James Buchanan.* Danbury, Conn.: Children's Press, 1988.

Buchanan, James. *Mr. Buchanan's Administration: On the Eve of the Rebellion.* Seattle: Digital Scanning, Inc., 2000.

Collins, David R. and Richard G. Young, ed. *James Buchanan: Fifteenth President of the United States.* Ada, Olka.: Garrett Educational Corporation, 1990.

Curtis, George T. *Life of James Buchanan.* Temecula, Calif.: Reprint Services Corporation, 1993.

DeGregorio, William A. *The Complete Book of U.S. Presidents.* New York: Wings Books, 1997.

Joseph, Paul. *James Buchanan.* Edina, Minn.: ABDO Publishing Company, 2000.

Klein, Philip S and Katherine E. Speirs, ed. *President James Buchanan: A President.* Newtown, Conn.: American Political Biography, 1995.

Steins, Richard. *Taylor, Fillmore, Pierce, & Buchanan.* Vero Beach, Fla.: Rourke Corporation, 1996.

Index